I Choose Gratitude

Stefanie Dunnigan & Tina Traina

Who?

The "I Choose" book series is created by teachers for teachers, students, and anyone looking to bring a little more peace, joy, and sense of purpose into their lives.

What?

Our book, "I Choose Gratitude," highlights the importance of a daily gratitude practice. Feeling grateful for the things that make us happy is easy but learning to accept challenges is a game changer.

By embracing life's obstacles, we can uncover the valuable lessons they hold. Gratitude creates space around and appreciation for challenges, big and small, making them all workable.

Why?

In life, we have choices. Some decisions are easy; some are difficult, while others are subconscious. We may notice our automatic reaction is to withdraw, fight, or freeze when faced with stressful situations.

These responses are sustainable for only so long until they leave us feeling depleted. Gratitude can be a bridge to help us shift from fear to love. Wouldn't it be nice to view life from a lens of love?

I CHOOSE GRATITUDE.
How about you?

When & Where?

Anytime.

Anywhere.

All the time.

Everywhere.

How?

This book is made with love and shared with love. We envision it as an uplifting read aloud or inspiring guide to accompany you on your life's journey. The messages can become daily reminders or the incentive to take a mindful moment.

Our watercolor illustrations are intended to evoke thoughts and ideas to help you visualize your future. They can also provide a backdrop to capture the mini meditations in your mind.

I Choose to

Greet each day with a smile
Recognize life's treasures
Appreciate the world around me
Take time to be thankful
Identify all that I have
Transform my thinking
Understand my self-worth
Discover my gifts
Embrace opportunities

because
I CHOOSE GRATITUDE.

GREET EACH DAY WITH A SMILE

Take time to be thankful

Identify all that you have

Every chance you get,

CHOOSE GRATITUDE.

Simple

yet

powerful

GRATITUDE PRACTICES

GREET EACH DAY WITH A SMILE

As you wake up in the morning,
take a deep breath, SMILE and
say THANK YOU out loud.
Bring to mind various things,
big and small,
for which you are
grateful.

RECOGNIZE LIFE'S TREASURES

It is easy to get caught up in life's
demands while walking through
the day unaware and on autopilot.
Take a moment to think about the
things that make you happy.

What do you cherish?

APPRECIATE THE WORLD AROUND YOU

Give yourself the gift of becoming aware of the present moment and look around you with new eyes. What do you notice?

What new appreciation arises?

TAKE TIME TO BE THANKFUL

We all get those intuitive feelings to reach out and thank someone. Sometimes we let that opportunity pass us by. Next time you get that gut feeling, practice taking action. Reach out and say thank you, even to yourself.

IDENTIFY ALL THAT YOU HAVE

Focus on what you have rather than what you lack. Practice feeling grateful for what you do have. As you increase your feelings of gratitude, you may notice that more opportunities for which to feel grateful will start to show up in your life.

TRANSFORM YOUR THINKING

In every situation, no matter how dark it may feel or be, there is something for which to be grateful. Practice reframing your mental narrative and shine a spotlight on gratitude. If you transform your thinking, you can transform your life.

UNDERSTAND YOUR SELF-WORTH

Many of us have limiting beliefs that tell us that we are not good enough in one way or another. Those beliefs are not telling us the truth. Be grateful for those limiting beliefs because they encourage us to dig deeper to find the truth and the truth is that YOU MATTER.

DISCOVER YOUR GIFTS

Connect with your inner wisdom that knows you already have everything you need. Tap into that wisdom. Think about what you like to do. What makes you light up? Go do that and share your strengths with the world because the world needs YOU to

shine your light.

EMBRACE OPPORTUNITIES

When we feel ungrateful, we tend to close ourselves off, letting opportunities pass us by. Yet, when we practice gratitude, we open ourselves up to endless possibilities. Practice embracing opportunities with an open and
grateful heart.

WE CHOOSE GRATITUDE.

How about you?

We've all heard that it takes 21 days to form a new habit.
Since it is important to make gratitude a daily practice,
we came up with a challenge:

FOCUS ON YOU FOR 22

The idea is to fill yourself up with gratitude so you can
then share it with others.

Look for our "I Choose Gratitude" journal to be your
companion and guide through the 22 days.
With practices and space to record your ideas, this journal
will help you develop an attitude of gratitude.

ARE YOU UP FOR THE CHALLENGE?

May you have a life full of gratitude and happiness. We hope you enjoyed reading our book as much as we loved creating it.

We invite you to share your experience reading "I Choose Gratitude." Please post a picture or kind word on our Facebook Page.
@IChooseBookSeries

With gratitude,

Stef and Tina

A bit about the authors

We have been friends since high school and enjoy creating together.

We are the authors and illustrators of "Travel Tails: All Bark and No Bite." Inspired by our dogs, we created the Travel Tails series to use with our students while focusing on literacy and character education.

Delving deeper into building good character for ourselves and our students, we have adopted a personal mindfulness practice that has transformed our lives.

Our
Classrooms

when we embody

Compassion
Acceptance
Responsibility &
Empathy
to
Nourish
Ourselves & Others
Worldwide!

We expanded our vision and created Classrooms C.A.R.E. N.O.W. which provides a framework to strengthen and highlight good character.

Please visit us at
http://www.traveltailsbooks.com/
https://www.classroomscarenow.com/

To empower ourselves and our children, we:

★ Promote awareness
★ Instill responsibility
★ Inspire action

Classrooms
C.A.R.E. N.O.W.

www.classroomscarenow.com

I have been on a personal journey of inner transformation. Seeing how it is inspiring my life and the lives of my students, I am committed to making this a life long journey. Classrooms CARE NOW and writing books are my way to share my learning with everyone and help others overcome the challenges we all face!

In working with Stefanie, I am learning to take mindful moments and express gratitude instead of viewing challenges through a lens of fear. I have begun to see how the positive energy is changing my life and inspiring me to continue on this path. I am truly grateful that Stef and I can embark on this mission together through writing our books and Classrooms CARE NOW.

Tina

For all who are looking to bring a little more peace, joy and sense of purpose into their lives.
-S & T

I Choose Gratitude

Text & illustrations copyright © 2018 Stefanie Dunnigan & Tina Traina

ISBN 978-0-9962796-1-1

The information in this book is true and complete to the best of our knowledge. All recommendations are made without guarantee on the part of the authors. The authors disclaim any liability in connection with use of this information.

All rights reserved. This book may not be reproduced in whole or in part in any form, or by any means, without express written permission from the publisher.

Published by:
Stefanie Dunnigan & Tina Traina
www.classroomscarenow.com
Savvy Scribblers, LLC

www.ingramcontent.com/pod-product-compliance
Lightning Source LLC
Chambersburg PA
CBHW061155010526
44118CB00027B/2985